W9-BGU-235

Date: 4/13/20

J BIO BUCHANAN
Gunderson, Megan M.,
James Buchanan /

The UNITED STATES PRESIDENTS

James BUCHANAN

Megan M. Gunderson

Big Buddy Books

An Imprint of Abdo Publishing
abdopublishing.com

abdopublishing.com

Published by Abdo Publishing, a division of ABDO, PO Box 398166, Minneapolis, Minnesota 55439.
Copyright © 2017 by Abdo Consulting Group, Inc. International copyrights reserved in all countries. No
part of this book may be reproduced in any form without written permission from the publisher. Big Buddy
Books™ is a trademark and logo of Abdo Publishing.

Printed in the United States of America, North Mankato, Minnesota
062016
092016

THIS BOOK CONTAINS
RECYCLED MATERIALS

Design: Sarah DeYoung, Mighty Media, Inc.
Production: Mighty Media, Inc.
Editor: Liz Salzmann
Cover Photograph: Getty
Interior Photographs: Alamy (pp. 7, 23, 29); Corbis (pp. 5, 27); Library of Congress (pp. 6, 7, 13, 15, 17,
    21, 25); Northwind (p. 9); Picture History (pp. 11, 19)

Cataloging-in-Publication Data

Names: Gunderson, Megan M., author.
Title: James Buchanan / by Megan M. Gunderson.
Description: Minneapolis, MN : Abdo Publishing, [2017] | Series: United States
    presidents | Includes bibliographical references and index.
Identifiers: LCCN 2015957272 | ISBN 9781680780840 (lib. bdg.) |
    ISBN 9781680775044 (ebook)
Subjects: LCSH: Buchanan, James, 1791-1868--Juvenile literature. | Presidents--
    United States--Biography--Juvenile literature. | United States--Politics and
    government--1857-1861--Juvenile literature.
Classification: DDC 973.6/8092 [B]--dc23
LC record available at http://lccn.loc.gov/2015957272

Contents

James Buchanan

James Buchanan served as the fifteenth US president. When he took office, he had already worked in **politics** for more than 40 years.

As president, Buchanan faced a troubled time in the nation's history. The Northern and Southern states were arguing over slavery. The country was about to come apart.

President Buchanan tried to keep the country together. But several Southern states left the Union. Soon after Buchanan left the White House, the **American Civil War** began.

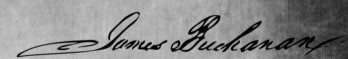

Timeline

1791

On April 23, James Buchanan was born in Cove Gap, Pennsylvania.

1834

Buchanan began serving in the US Senate.

1814

Buchanan was elected to the Pennsylvania House of **Representatives**.

1845

Under President James K. Polk, Buchanan became **secretary of state**.

1857
Buchanan became the fifteenth US president.

1853
President Franklin Pierce appointed Buchanan **minister** to Great Britain.

1868
On June 1, James Buchanan died at Wheatland.

Young James

James Buchanan was born in Cove Gap, Pennsylvania, on April 23, 1791. James's father was a successful storekeeper and landowner.

James attended college in Carlisle, Pennsylvania. He **graduated** in 1809.

The college James attended was Dickinson College. It is named for Pennsylvania governor John Dickinson.

Entering Politics

James briefly served in the **War of 1812**. He helped **defend** Baltimore, Maryland. Soon afterward, he began working in **politics**.

Buchanan's first political position was in the Pennsylvania House of **Representatives**. He served from 1814 to 1816.

Buchanan was elected to the US House of Representatives in 1820. He served five terms from 1821 to 1831.

★ DID YOU KNOW? ★

James Buchanan had ten brothers and sisters.

Buchanan got his love of books and country from his mother.

Foreign Service

In the early 1830s, President Andrew Jackson made Buchanan **minister** to Russia. As minister, Buchanan arranged the first trade agreement between Russia and the United States.

After returning from Russia, Buchanan was elected to the US Senate. He worked there from 1834 to 1845. Senator Buchanan served as head of the Committee on Foreign Relations. This group works with the governments of other countries.

Buchanan gained important experience working in different countries. This helped prepare him for being secretary of state and president.

In 1845, Buchanan became President James K. Polk's **secretary of state**. At the time, the United States had problems to settle with other countries. As secretary, Buchanan helped settle a border disagreement with England over the Oregon Territory.

Buchanan also tried to settle a border argument with Mexico. But, his attempts failed. The disagreement led to the Mexican War. The United States and Mexico fought the war from 1846 to 1848.

★ DID YOU KNOW? ★

James Buchanan was called "Old Buck."

James K. Polk
was president
from 1845
to 1849.

A New Position

When President Polk's term ended, Buchanan stopped being **secretary of state**. He had recently joined the **Democratic** Party. Now, Buchanan hoped the Democrats would choose him to run for president in the 1852 election.

However, the Democrats chose Franklin Pierce instead. Buchanan **supported** Pierce. Pierce won the election. Then in 1853, he made Buchanan **minister** to Great Britain.

While minister, Buchanan tried to help the United States gain Cuba.

Election of 1856

In 1856, the **Democrats** chose Buchanan to run for president. Buchanan ran against Millard Fillmore and John C. Frémont. Buchanan won the election.

On March 4, 1857, Buchanan was **inaugurated**. He became president as the argument over slavery reached its high point. Still, Buchanan hoped the problem would be settled in court.

★ SUPREME COURT ★
APPOINTMENTS

Nathan Clifford: 1858

John Wood took a picture
of Buchanan entering
office. It was the first
picture ever taken of a
president's inauguration.

Dred Scott

Soon after Buchanan took office, the US **Supreme Court** decided the *Dred Scott* case. Dred Scott was a Missouri slave. He had traveled with his owner to Illinois and the Wisconsin Territory.

After returning to Missouri, Scott argued in court for his freedom. He had lived in free areas. So, Scott thought he should be a free man.

On March 6, 1857, the Supreme Court ruled against Scott. But many in the North did not **support** the *Dred Scott* decision.

Two months
after losing
the court case,
Dred Scott
was freed
by his owner.

Bleeding Kansas

When Buchanan took office, the Kansas Territory had two governments. The government in Lecompton **supported** slavery. The Topeka government was against it. This fight over slavery became known as "Bleeding Kansas."

In 1857, the Kansas voters passed the Lecompton **Constitution**, which allowed slavery. The Senate approved it. However, the House did not. Buchanan supported the constitution because it had passed legally.

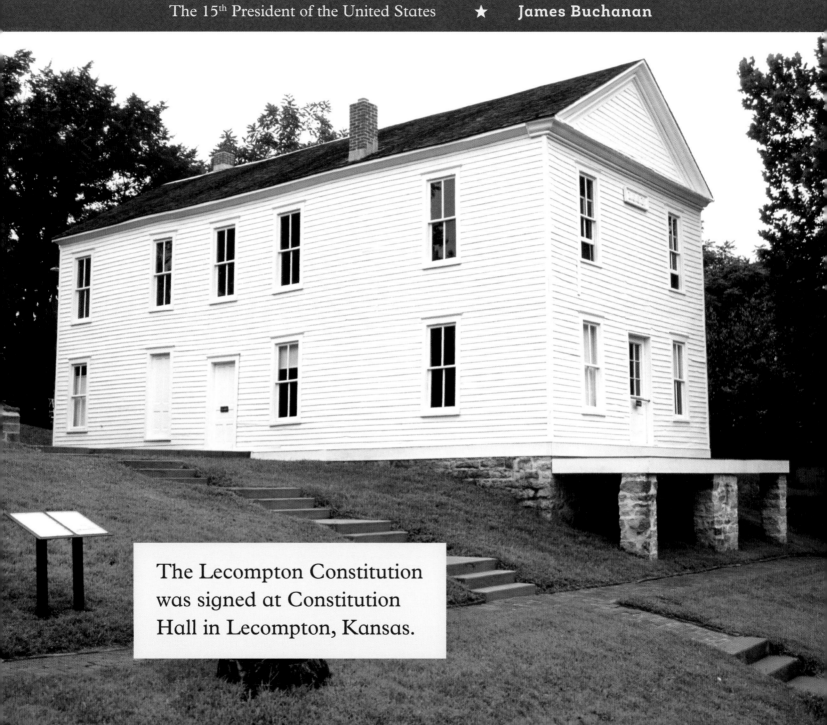

The Lecompton Constitution was signed at Constitution Hall in Lecompton, Kansas.

Harpers Ferry

Buchanan's slavery problems continued. John Brown was leading a **rebellion** against slavery. In October 1859, Brown seized the US weapons storehouse at Harpers Ferry, Virginia.

National troops arrived at Harpers Ferry on October 17. They fought Brown and his followers. Brown was hanged for **treason** on December 2.

This event caused more problems between the North and South. Northerners were upset that Buchanan **defended** slavery and the South.

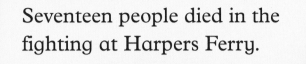

Seventeen people died in the fighting at Harpers Ferry.

Divided Nation

During Buchanan's last four months in office, seven Southern states **seceded**. They started their own country called the **Confederate** States of America.

In January 1861, Buchanan sent supplies to **Fort** Sumter in South Carolina. This US fort was now in Confederate territory. Confederate forces surrounded the fort. They forced the supply ships to turn back. Before Buchanan could try to help the fort again, his term ended.

PRESIDENT BUCHANAN'S CABINET

March 4, 1857–March 4, 1861

★ **STATE:** Lewis Cass,
Jeremiah S. Black (from December 17, 1860)

★ **TREASURY:** Howell Cobb,
Philip F. Thomas (from December 12, 1860),
John A. Dix (from January 15, 1861)

★ **WAR:** John B. Floyd

★ **NAVY:** Isaac Toucey

★ **ATTORNEY GENERAL:** Jeremiah S. Black,
Edwin M. Stanton (from December 22, 1860)

★ **INTERIOR:** Jacob Thompson

Retirement

On March 4, 1861, Buchanan left office. He returned to his home near Lancaster, Pennsylvania. Soon after, the **American Civil War** began. Buchanan strongly **supported** the Union. At the time, many people blamed Buchanan for not preventing the war.

James Buchanan died on June 1, 1868. Today, he is remembered for trying to stop the war in the hopes of peace.

Buchanan's home is called Wheatland. It is now a historic site, which people can visit.

Office of the President

Branches of Government

The US government has three branches. They are the executive, legislative, and judicial branches. Each branch has some power over the others. This is called a system of checks and balances.

★ **Executive Branch**

The executive branch enforces laws. It is made up of the president, the vice president, and the president's cabinet. The president represents the United States around the world. He or she also signs bills into law and leads the military.

★ **Legislative Branch**

The legislative branch makes laws, maintains the military, and regulates trade. It also has the power to declare war. This branch includes the Senate and the House of Representatives. Together, these two houses form Congress.

★ **Judicial Branch**

The judicial branch interprets laws. It is made up of district courts, courts of appeals, and the Supreme Court. District courts try cases. Sometimes people disagree with a trial's outcome. Then he or she may appeal. If a court of appeals supports the ruling, a person may appeal to the Supreme Court.

Qualifications for Office

To be president, a candidate must be at least 35 years old. The person must be a natural-born US citizen. He or she must also have lived in the United States for at least 14 years.

Electoral College

The US presidential election is an indirect election. Voters from each state choose electors. These electors represent their state in the Electoral College. Each elector has one electoral vote. Electors cast their vote for the candidate with the highest number of votes from people in their state. A candidate must receive the majority of Electoral College votes to win.

Term of Office

Each president may be elected to two four-year terms. The presidential election is held on the Tuesday after the first Monday in November. The president is sworn in on January 20 of the following year. At that time, he or she takes the oath of office.
It states:

> I do solemnly swear (or affirm) that I will faithfully execute the office of President of the United States, and will to the best of my ability, preserve, protect and defend the Constitution of the United States.

31

Line of Succession

The Presidential Succession Act of 1947 states who becomes president if the president cannot serve. The vice president is first in the line. Next are the Speaker of the House and the President Pro Tempore of the Senate. It may happen that none of these individuals is able to serve. Then the office falls to the president's cabinet members. They would take office in the order in which each department was created:

Secretary of State

Secretary of the Treasury

Secretary of Defense

Attorney General

Secretary of the Interior

Secretary of Agriculture

Secretary of Commerce

Secretary of Labor

Secretary of Health and Human Services

Secretary of Housing and Urban Development

Secretary of Transportation

Secretary of Energy

Secretary of Education

Secretary of Veterans Affairs

Secretary of Homeland Security

Benefits

★ While in office, the president receives a salary. It is $400,000 per year. He or she lives in the White House. The president also has 24-hour Secret Service protection.

★ The president may travel on a Boeing 747 jet. This special jet is called Air Force One. It can hold 70 passengers. It has kitchens, a dining room, sleeping areas, and more. Air Force One can fly halfway around the world before needing to refuel. It can even refuel in flight!

★ When the president travels by car, he or she uses Cadillac One. It is a Cadillac Deville that has been modified. The car has heavy armor and communications systems. The president may even take Cadillac One along when visiting other countries.

★ The president also travels on a helicopter. It is called Marine One. It may also be taken along when the president visits other countries.

★ Sometimes the president needs to get away with family and friends. Camp David is the official presidential retreat. It is located in Maryland. The US Navy maintains the retreat. The US Marine Corps keeps it secure. The camp offers swimming, tennis, golf, and hiking.

★ When the president leaves office, he or she receives lifetime Secret Service protection. He or she also receives a yearly pension of $203,700. The former president also receives money for office space, supplies, and staff.

PRESIDENTS AND THEIR TERMS

PRESIDENT	PARTY	TOOK OFFICE	LEFT OFFICE	TERMS SERVED	VICE PRESIDENT
George Washington	None	April 30, 1789	March 4, 1797	Two	John Adams
John Adams	Federalist	March 4, 1797	March 4, 1801	One	Thomas Jefferson
Thomas Jefferson	Democratic-Republican	March 4, 1801	March 4, 1809	Two	Aaron Burr, George Clinton
James Madison	Democratic-Republican	March 4, 1809	March 4, 1817	Two	George Clinton, Elbridge Gerry
James Monroe	Democratic-Republican	March 4, 1817	March 4, 1825	Two	Daniel D. Tompkins
John Quincy Adams	Democratic-Republican	March 4, 1825	March 4, 1829	One	John C. Calhoun
Andrew Jackson	Democrat	March 4, 1829	March 4, 1837	Two	John C. Calhoun, Martin Van Buren
Martin Van Buren	Democrat	March 4, 1837	March 4, 1841	One	Richard M. Johnson
William H. Harrison	Whig	March 4, 1841	April 4, 1841	Died During First Term	John Tyler
John Tyler	Whig	April 6, 1841	March 4, 1845	Completed Harrison's Term	Office Vacant
James K. Polk	Democrat	March 4, 1845	March 4, 1849	One	George M. Dallas
Zachary Taylor	Whig	March 5, 1849	July 9, 1850	Died During First Term	Millard Fillmore

PRESIDENT	PARTY	TOOK OFFICE	LEFT OFFICE	TERMS SERVED	VICE PRESIDENT
Millard Fillmore	Whig	July 10, 1850	March 4, 1853	Completed Taylor's Term	Office Vacant
Franklin Pierce	Democrat	March 4, 1853	March 4, 1857	One	William R.D. King
James Buchanan	Democrat	March 4, 1857	March 4, 1861	One	John C. Breckinridge
Abraham Lincoln	Republican	March 4, 1861	April 15, 1865	Served One Term, Died During Second Term	Hannibal Hamlin, Andrew Johnson
Andrew Johnson	Democrat	April 15, 1865	March 4, 1869	Completed Lincoln's Second Term	Office Vacant
Ulysses S. Grant	Republican	March 4, 1869	March 4, 1877	Two	Schuyler Colfax, Henry Wilson
Rutherford B. Hayes	Republican	March 3, 1877	March 4, 1881	One	William A. Wheeler
James A. Garfield	Republican	March 4, 1881	September 19, 1881	Died During First Term	Chester Arthur
Chester Arthur	Republican	September 20, 1881	March 4, 1885	Completed Garfield's Term	Office Vacant
Grover Cleveland	Democrat	March 4, 1885	March 4, 1889	One	Thomas A. Hendricks
Benjamin Harrison	Republican	March 4, 1889	March 4, 1893	One	Levi P. Morton
Grover Cleveland	Democrat	March 4, 1893	March 4, 1897	One	Adlai E. Stevenson
William McKinley	Republican	March 4, 1897	September 14, 1901	Served One Term, Died During Second Term	Garret A. Hobart, Theodore Roosevelt

PRESIDENT	PARTY	TOOK OFFICE	LEFT OFFICE	TERMS SERVED	VICE PRESIDENT
Theodore Roosevelt	Republican	September 14, 1901	March 4, 1909	Completed McKinley's Second Term, Served One Term	Office Vacant, Charles Fairbanks
William Taft	Republican	March 4, 1909	March 4, 1913	One	James S. Sherman
Woodrow Wilson	Democrat	March 4, 1913	March 4, 1921	Two	Thomas R. Marshall
Warren G. Harding	Republican	March 4, 1921	August 2, 1923	Died During First Term	Calvin Coolidge
Calvin Coolidge	Republican	August 3, 1923	March 4, 1929	Completed Harding's Term, Served One Term	Office Vacant, Charles Dawes
Herbert Hoover	Republican	March 4, 1929	March 4, 1933	One	Charles Curtis
Franklin D. Roosevelt	Democrat	March 4, 1933	April 12, 1945	Served Three Terms, Died During Fourth Term	John Nance Garner, Henry A. Wallace, Harry S. Truman
Harry S. Truman	Democrat	April 12, 1945	January 20, 1953	Completed Roosevelt's Fourth Term, Served One Term	Office Vacant, Alben Barkley
Dwight D. Eisenhower	Republican	January 20, 1953	January 20, 1961	Two	Richard Nixon
John F. Kennedy	Democrat	January 20, 1961	November 22, 1963	Died During First Term	Lyndon B. Johnson
Lyndon B. Johnson	Democrat	November 22, 1963	January 20, 1969	Completed Kennedy's Term, Served One Term	Office Vacant, Hubert H. Humphrey
Richard Nixon	Republican	January 20, 1969	August 9, 1974	Completed First Term, Resigned During Second Term	Spiro T. Agnew, Gerald Ford

PRESIDENT	PARTY	TOOK OFFICE	LEFT OFFICE	TERMS SERVED	VICE PRESIDENT
Gerald Ford	Republican	August 9, 1974	January 20, 1977	Completed Nixon's Second Term	Nelson A. Rockefeller
Jimmy Carter	Democrat	January 20, 1977	January 20, 1981	One	Walter Mondale
Ronald Reagan	Republican	January 20, 1981	January 20, 1989	Two	George H.W. Bush
George H.W. Bush	Republican	January 20, 1989	January 20, 1993	One	Dan Quayle
Bill Clinton	Democrat	January 20, 1993	January 20, 2001	Two	Al Gore
George W. Bush	Republican	January 20, 2001	January 20, 2009	Two	Dick Cheney
Barack Obama	Democrat	January 20, 2009	January 20, 2017	Two	Joe Biden

"We ought to do justice in a kindly spirit to all nations and require justice from them in return." James Buchanan

★ WRITE TO THE PRESIDENT ★

You may write to the president at:
The White House
1600 Pennsylvania Avenue NW
Washington, DC 20500

You may e-mail the president at:
comments@whitehouse.gov

37

Glossary

American Civil War—the war between the Northern and Southern states from 1861 to 1865.

Confederate—of or related to the group of Southern states that declared independence during the American Civil War.

constitution (kahnt-stuh-TOO-shuhn)—the basic laws that govern a country or a state.

defend—to fight danger in order to keep safe or to argue in favor of an opinion or action.

Democrat—a member of the Democratic political party.

fort—a building with strong walls to guard against enemies.

graduate (GRA-juh-wayt)—to complete a level of schooling.

inaugurate—to swear into a political office.

minister—a type of government official.

politics—the art or science of government. Something referring to politics is political. A person who is active in politics is a politician.

rebellion—open fighting against one's government or ruler.

representative—someone chosen in an election to act or speak for the people who voted for him or her.

secede—to officially withdraw from a group or organization.

secretary of state—a member of the president's cabinet who handles relations with other countries.

support—to believe in or be in favor of something.

Supreme Court—the highest, most powerful court of a nation or a state.

treason—a crime committed against one's own country or government.

War of 1812—a war between the United States and England from 1812 to 1815.

★ WEBSITES ★

To learn more about the US Presidents, visit **booklinks.abdopublishing.com**. These links are routinely monitored and updated to provide the most current information available.

Index